AF270354

Vitamins
as Necessary Nutrients

BY ASHLEY GISH

Kids Core

An Imprint of Abdo Publishing
abdobooks.com

abdobooks.com

Published by Abdo Publishing, a division of ABDO, PO Box 398166, Minneapolis, Minnesota 55439. Copyright © 2023 by Abdo Consulting Group, Inc. International copyrights reserved in all countries. No part of this book may be reproduced in any form without written permission from the publisher. Kids Core™ is a trademark and logo of Abdo Publishing.

Printed in the United States of America, North Mankato, Minnesota
102022
012023

THIS BOOK CONTAINS
RECYCLED MATERIALS

Cover Photo: Shutterstock Images
Interior Photos: iStockphoto, 4–5, 6, 25; Africa Studio/Shutterstock Images, 7, 10, 19; Antonio Diaz/iStockphoto, 9; Shutterstock Images, 12–13, 15, 22 (salmon), 22 (almonds), 22 (strawberries), 26, 28 (top), 28 (bottom), 29 (top); Stefanie Metzger/iStockphoto, 16; Professional Studio Images/iStockphoto, 18; Ekaterina Minaeva/Shutterstock Images, 20–21; Anna Zabella/Shutterstock Images, 22 (carrots), 22 (broccoli), 22 (bananas); Ivan Kislitsin/Shutterstock Images, 23; Karepa Stock/Shutterstock Images, 29 (bottom)

Editor: Amanda Lanser
Series Designer: Layna Darling

Library of Congress Control Number: 2022940654

Publisher's Cataloging-in-Publication Data

Names: Gish, Ashley, author.
Title: Vitamins as necessary nutrients / by Ashley Gish
Description: Minneapolis, Minnesota: Abdo Publishing, 2023 | Series: Necessary nutrients | Includes online resources and index.
Identifiers: ISBN 9781098290054 (lib. bdg.) | ISBN 9781098275259 (ebook)
Subjects: LCSH: Vitamins--Juvenile literature. | Vitamins in human nutrition--Juvenile literature. | Vitamin deficiency--Juvenile literature. | Nutrition--Health aspects--Juvenile literature.
Classification: DDC 613.2--dc23

CONTENTS

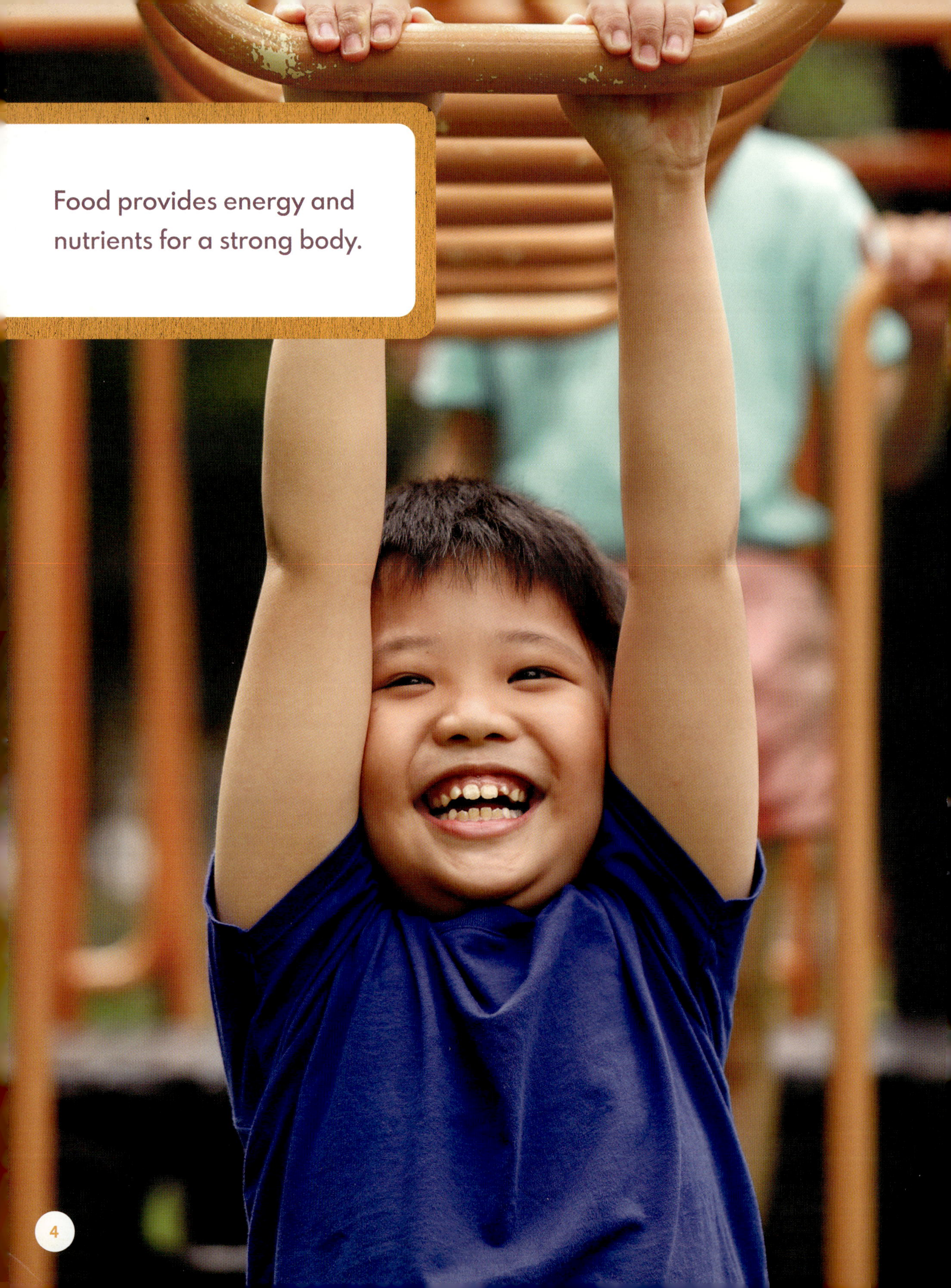

Food provides energy and
nutrients for a strong body.

Very Important Vitamins

It was a spring day. Mason ran out of his classroom for recess. The damp soil made his shoes slippery. He started to climb the jungle gym. Toward the top, Mason slipped. He fell off the jungle gym. His arm hurt a lot.

Vitamin D helps strengthen bones.

The nurse told him his arm was broken. Mason's mom picked him up. She took him to the doctor.

Mason's doctor told him he needed to wear a cast. Mason needed to eat foods with **calcium** and vitamin D. He learned these substances

Orange juice sometimes has calcium and vitamin D added.

Boosted Food

Some foods have vitamins added to them. They are more nutritious than the same foods without added vitamins. Milk, soy milk, and bread often have added vitamins. So do breakfast cereals and juices.

build strong bones. That night, he had a big glass of milk with dinner. Milk naturally contains calcium. Vitamin D is added to milk.

This makes it even more nutritious. Mason felt good. He was helping his body heal.

Vitamins Are Necessary

Vitamins are nutrients. Nutrients are substances in food. The body needs nutrients to grow and stay healthy. The human body cannot make many vitamins. People must eat wholesome, fresh foods to get them. Not eating the right amounts of vitamins can lead to illness.

Vitamins are tiny substances. They are visible only through a microscope. But they each play an important role in the body. Vitamin K helps blood clot. This stops a cut from bleeding.

Vitamin K helps cuts stop bleeding.

Vitamin C helps heal cuts and scrapes. Thiamin is one of the B vitamins. It keeps the heart beating strong.

Fresh foods, such as vegetables, contain lots of vitamins.

Some vitamins, such as vitamin D, may even help people feel happier. The sun provides vitamin D. Skin soaks up sunlight. It makes vitamin D from it. Foods also contain vitamin D.

People get most of the vitamins they need from food. Different foods contain different vitamins. Each vitamin performs a different role in the body. It is important to eat a variety of foods. This helps the body get all the vitamins it needs.

Further Evidence

Look at the website below. Does it give any new evidence to support Chapter One?

Broken Bones

abdocorelibrary.com/vitamins-as-necessary-nutrients

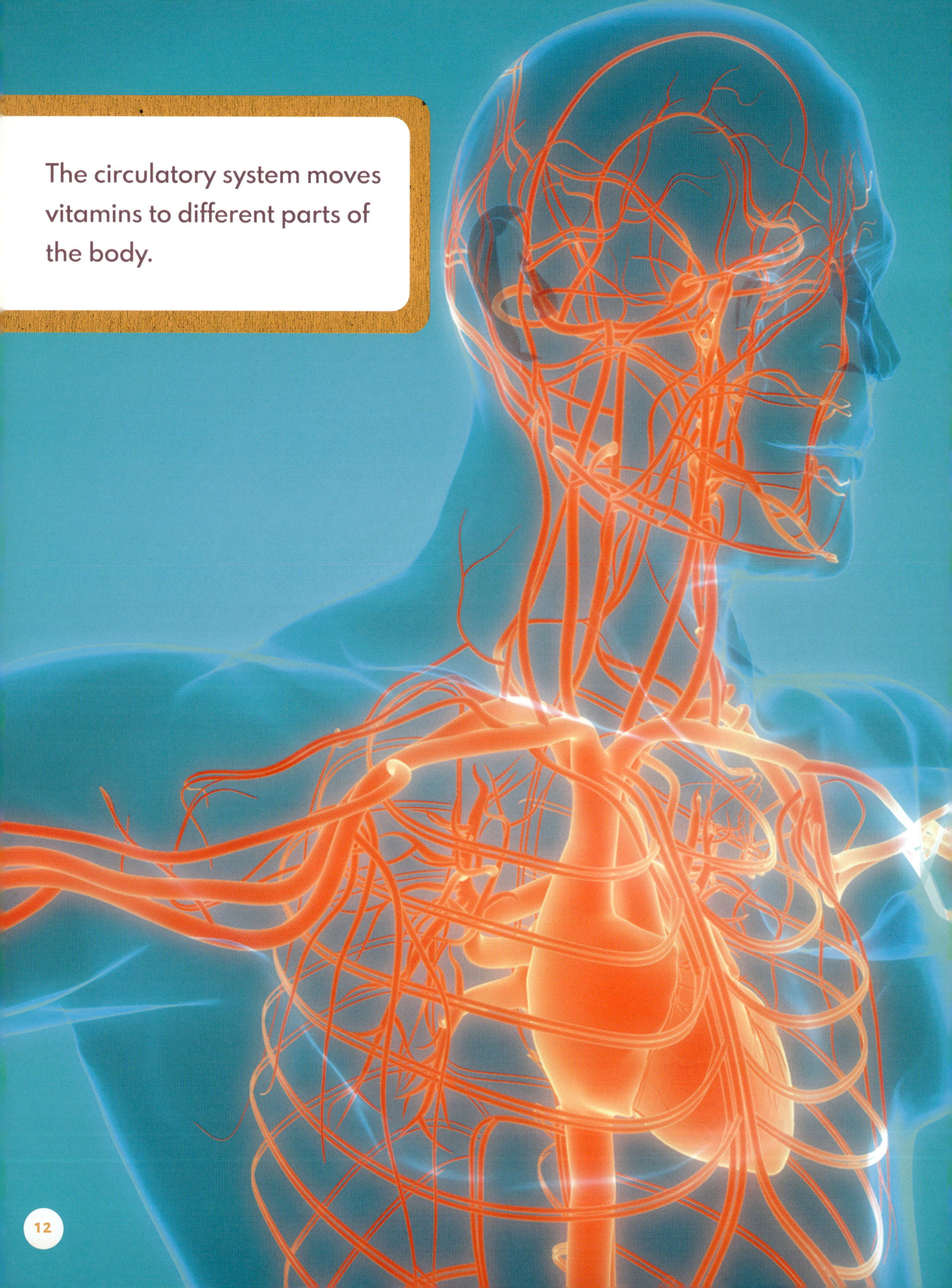

The circulatory system moves vitamins to different parts of the body.

CHAPTER 2

What the Body Needs

The body uses 13 vitamins. These vitamins are divided into two groups. Some are fat **soluble**. Others are water soluble. The **circulatory system** carries vitamins throughout the body.

Fat-Soluble Vitamins

The body absorbs fat-soluble vitamins with the fats from food. They are stored in fat until the body needs them. The body can store fat-soluble vitamins for up to six months. The body may store too much of a fat-soluble vitamin. This can cause illness.

Vitamins A, D, E, and K are fat-soluble vitamins. Vitamin A improves eyesight. It also helps the body grow. It boosts the immune system. A healthy immune system fights off illnesses. Bell peppers, sweet potatoes, and carrots contain vitamin A.

Vitamin D builds strong bones and teeth. Sunlight and some foods provide vitamin D. It can be found in salmon, sardines, and eggs.

Orange peppers contain vitamin A.

Some mushrooms grown under special lights have vitamin D too.

Vitamin E protects the body from having too many free radicals. These substances protect the body from illness. But too many free radicals leads to diseases.

Almonds are a great source of vitamin E.

Vitamin E also keeps the heart healthy. Vitamin E is found in vegetable oils, nuts, and grains.

The last fat-soluble vitamin is vitamin K. Without vitamin K, an injury may not stop bleeding. Leafy greens, blueberries, and dairy foods are great sources of vitamin K.

Water-Soluble Vitamins

Water-soluble vitamins enter the circulatory system through the gut. The body does not store water-soluble vitamins. Extra ones are released from the body in urine. Vitamin C and the eight B vitamins are water soluble.

Vitamin C helps heal cuts. It builds strong **cell** walls. It helps prevent **heart disease**. Vitamin C is found in many fruits and vegetables, including oranges and tomatoes.

C Is Not for *Cold*

Some people believe that vitamin C prevents the common cold. But experts disagree. Vitamin C can shorten the time a person is sick by about one day. But it does not keep people from catching colds. The best ways to keep from catching colds are washing hands, getting plenty of rest, and drinking enough water.

Strawberries contain lots of vitamin C.

There are eight B vitamins. Some B vitamins help create healthy blood. Others protect the body from disease. Still others help break down food into energy. The B vitamins are found in a variety of foods. Whole grains and beans contain some B vitamins. So do many fruits and vegetables. Dairy foods, meat, poultry, and fish contain some B vitamins too.

Milk is a good source of B vitamins.

Getting enough of all 13 vitamins helps the body function. They help people stay healthy.

Explore Online

Visit the website below. What new information did you learn about vitamins that wasn't in Chapter Two?

Nutrition—Science Trek

abdocorelibrary.com/vitamins-as -necessary-nutrients

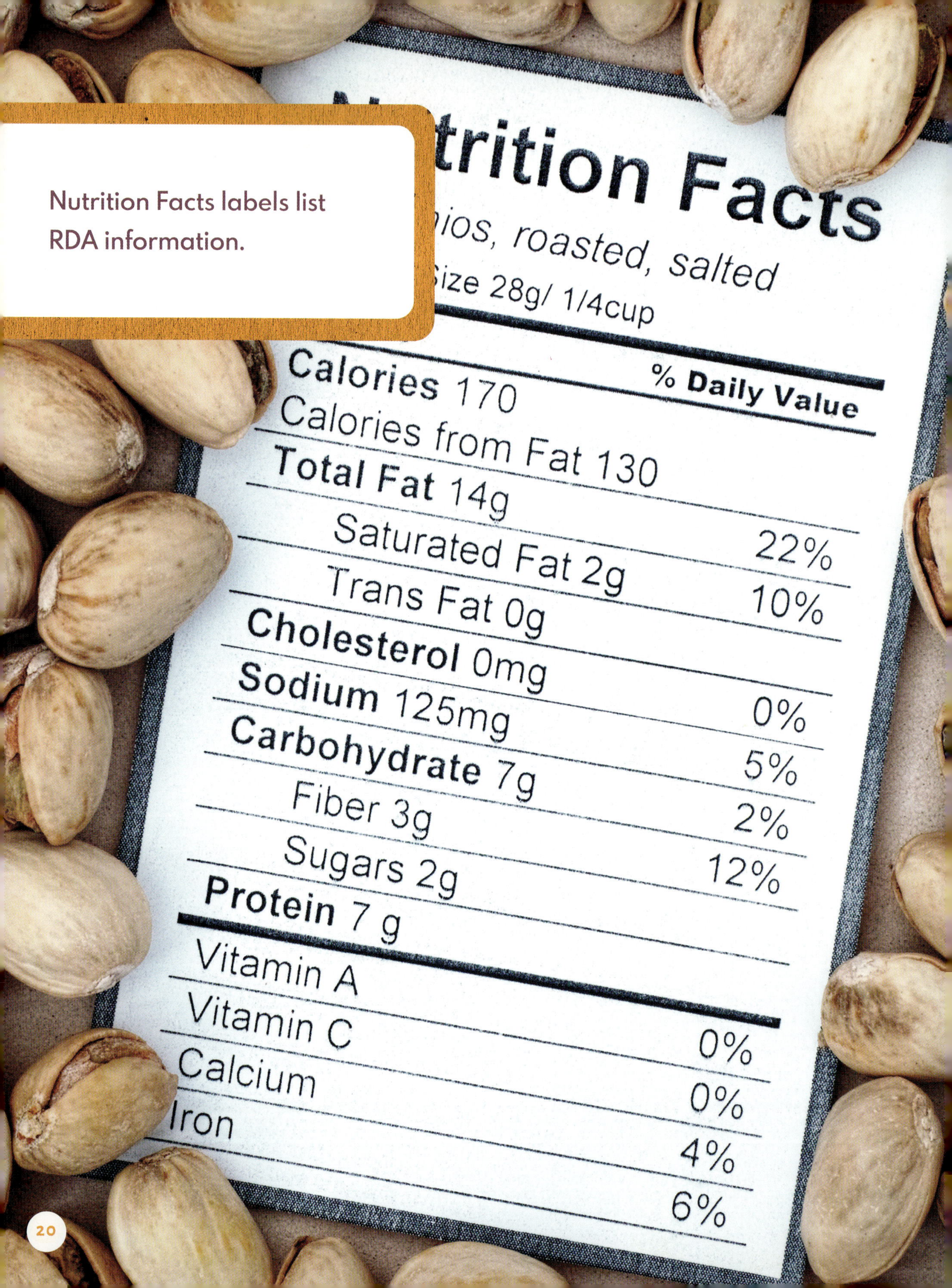

Nutrition Facts labels list RDA information.

CHAPTER 3

Getting Enough Vitamins

Experts research how much of each vitamin the body needs. They have determined the amounts someone needs to get every day. This daily amount is called the Recommended Dietary Allowance (RDA).

Vitamins in Whole Foods

Baby Carrots
8 pieces
65% RDA
Vitamin A

Salmon
3-ounce fillet
56% RDA
Vitamin D

Almonds
1/4 cup
61% RDA
Vitamin E

Broccoli
1/2 cup
37% RDA
Vitamin K

Strawberries
1/2 cup
47% RDA
Vitamin C

Bananas
1 medium
25% RDA
Vitamin B

People should eat a variety of whole foods every day. They have many nutrients, including vitamins.

The body needs the right amount of vitamins. Getting too much can be harmful. Too much vitamin A can weaken bones. They may

break easily. Vitamin D helps build bones. But too much can cause calcium to harden other parts of the body, such as the heart and kidneys. A person should use the RDA to get the right amount of vitamins.

Labels list the vitamins in packaged foods. They show how much of the RDA the food contains.

Supplements also contain vitamins. Sometimes they contain more than the RDA.

This is not usually harmful. The stomach breaks down supplements before they reach the gut. For this reason, not all vitamins in supplements reach the circulatory system. Fresh foods should always be the number one source of vitamins. Vitamins are naturally present in these foods. Foods provide other important nutrients too.

Vitamin C on the High Seas

Not getting enough vitamin C can cause scurvy. This disease can make a person's teeth fall out. It also causes pain in the arms and legs. These symptoms were common among sailors. In the 1700s, the British navy found a solution. Fresh fruit cured and prevented scurvy.

Vitamins help the body grow strong and healthy.

Eating a wide variety of foods helps people get enough vitamins.

However, not all foods are nutritious. Fast foods do not contain many vitamins. These include pizza and french fries. Eating these foods often can lead to health problems. People may develop heart disease and other illnesses. People do not need to stop eating these foods completely. It is OK to eat fast foods sometimes.

Eating many different types of foods will help someone get a variety of vitamins. That way, a person can get all 13 vitamins the body needs!

Primary Source

In her book on vitamins, **dietician** Mascha Davis writes about getting vitamins from food:

> In short, the best way to get more energy, a stronger immune system, glowing skin, and overall better health is through the foods you eat, not the pills you take.

Source: Mascha Davis. *Eat Your Vitamins: Your Guide to Using Natural Foods to Get the Vitamins, Minerals, and Nutrients Your Body Needs.* Adams Media, 2020, p. 6.

Point of View

What is the author's point of view on this topic? What is your point of view? Write a short essay about how they are similar and different.

Nutrient Jobs

Vitamin D builds strong bones.

- Salmon
- Tuna
- Egg yolk

Vitamin K helps blood clot.

- Kale
- Spinach
- Brussels sprouts

Vitamin A improves eyesight.

- Sweet potatoes

- Red bell peppers

- Carrots

Vitamin C prevents damage to cells.

- Broccoli

- Oranges

- Strawberries

Glossary

calcium
a nutrient that builds and maintains strong bones

cell
the smallest and most basic unit of life

circulatory system
the system that delivers oxygen and nutrients to all parts of the body

dietician
someone who helps people make nutritious eating choices

heart disease
any of four diseases that weaken and damage the heart

soluble
able to be broken into tiny pieces and mixed into a particular substance, such as fat or water

supplements
pills, gummies, or liquids that provide vitamins and other nutrients

Online Resources

To learn more about vitamins as necessary nutrients, visit our free resource websites below.

Visit **abdocorelibrary.com** or scan this QR code for free Common Core resources for teachers and students, including vetted activities, multimedia, and booklinks, for deeper subject comprehension.

Visit **abdobooklinks.com** or scan this QR code for free additional online weblinks for further learning. These links are routinely monitored and updated to provide the most current information available.

Learn More

Golkar, Golriz. *The Immune System*. Abdo, 2023.

The Healthy Junior Chef Cookbook. Weldon Owen, 2020.

Troup, Roxanne. *The Circulatory System*. Abdo, 2023.

Index

About the Author

Ashley Gish earned her degree in creative writing from Minnesota State University, Mankato. She has authored more than 60 juvenile nonfiction books. Ashley lives happily in Rochester, Minnesota, with her husband, daughter, dog, cat, and three chickens.